TRAIN 'EM UP

ALL ABOARD!

RAIN 'EM UP

tell me about

BAPTISM

created by
STEPHEN ELKINS

illustrated by
RUTH ZEGLIN & SIMON TAYLOR-KIELTY

Tyndale House Publishers, Inc.
Carol Stream, Illinois

wonder
kids
Songs to Inspire Faith

choo choo
choo choo!
choo choo!

ALL ABOARD!

All aboard the Gospel train!

Get on Board, Little Children

FIND THIS SONG on the CD

The gospel train is comin'
The wheels go 'round and 'round
We're training up the children
So they'll be heaven bound

Chorus
Get on board, little children
Get on board, little children
Get on board, little children
There's room for many a-more

Hear that train a-comin'
Comin' down the track
I'll be getting on it
And won't be lookin' back

Repeat chorus

You won't need a penny
To ride this glorious train
Just give your heart to Jesus
And ride away with Him

Repeat chorus

3

Have you ever wondered what

BAPTISM is?

welcome to
BIBLE LAND

Yes, I have!
What **is** BAPTISM?

We're off to
DISCOVERY LAND
to find the answer.

5

Let's discover what the Bible says about **BAPTISM.**

1 Mile

DISCOVERY LAND

Some people think baptism has some special POWER.

The Bible says baptism is only "SHOW AND TELL."

We use water to show and tell others

WE LOVE JESUS!

TICKET

BAPTISM IS USING WATER TO SAY, "I LOVE JESUS!"

ALL ABOARD!

8

WHAT IS BAPTISM?

Baptism is like "show and tell." Being dipped in the water has no special power. It simply SHOWS God that you choose to follow Jesus. And it TELLS others that your life has been changed by Him. By being baptized you say, "I am a brand-new person!"

Baptism has no power to change you. Only Jesus can do that. But baptism SHOWS AND TELLS the world that you love Jesus!

* * *

For it is by grace you have been saved, through faith—and this is not from yourselves, it is the gift of God—not by works, so that no one can boast.

EPHESIANS 2:8-9, NIV

BAPTISM shows and tells the world you love Jesus.

WHY DO WE GET BAPTIZED? Baptism begins with the letter B. So does the word **BEGINNING.** Baptism marks a new beginning for those who trust Jesus.

We get baptized for two important reasons. First, it is a command of Jesus. He was baptized. So were His disciples. Secondly, this little three-second "show and tell" called baptism tells the world that you are beginning a new way of life with Jesus.

. . . .

Therefore, go and make disciples of all the nations, baptizing them. **MATTHEW 28:19**

Any time is the **RIGHT TIME** to be **BAPTIZED!**

WHEN DO WE GET BAPTIZED?

Baptism marks the beginning of a new life with Jesus. That's why you should be baptized soon after you decide to follow Jesus.

You don't have to wait until you're older or a "better Christian." The Bible says Paul was a terrible person. He was mean to Christians and put them in prison! But when Paul decided to follow Jesus, he was baptized immediately.

When you give your heart to Jesus and decide to follow Him, no need to wait! Any time is the right time to be baptized.

. . . .

You were called to . . . one Lord, one faith, one baptism; one God and Father of all.

EPHESIANS 4:4-6, NIV

14

WHERE DO WE GET BAPTIZED? All you need is water! It can be in your church's baptismal, or a lake, or a swimming pool! This short play takes only a minute to perform. Here's what the play is about:

- Jesus died on the cross to take away our sins.
- He was buried in a tomb.

When we go under the water, we show what Jesus did. He was buried. But three days later, Jesus arose. He was alive again. When we come up out of the water, we show that Jesus is alive!

. . . .

For you were buried with Christ when you were baptized. And with him you were raised to new life because you trusted the mighty power of God.
COLOSSIANS 2:12

WHO GETS BAPTIZED? When we decide to follow Jesus, it means we want to do the things He taught us to do. The Bible tells us that Jesus was baptized. He asked all His disciples to be baptized too. And He asked His followers to go, make more disciples, and baptize them.

It's pretty clear that people who love Jesus and choose to follow Him should be baptized.

....

John baptized him in the Jordan River. As Jesus came up out of the water, he saw the heavens splitting apart and the Holy Spirit descending on him like a dove. And a voice from heaven said, "You are my dearly loved Son, and you bring me great joy." **MARK 1:9-11**

THE BAPTISM OF JESUS

WE READ IN THE BIBLE about a man called John the Baptizer. And as you might expect, he baptized many people.

One day, Jesus came to be baptized. John was confused. Jesus didn't need to be baptized. He was perfect! But Jesus wanted everyone to see that baptism is important! It is a "show and tell" that says, "I love the Lord!"

STORY JUNCTION

His Father in heaven
was pleased!

19

FIND THIS SONG on the CD

I HAVE DECIDED TO FOLLOW JESUS

I have decided to follow Jesus
I have decided to follow Jesus
I have decided to follow Jesus
No turning back, no turning back

The world behind me, the cross before me
The world behind me, the cross before me
The world behind me, the cross before me
No turning back, no turning back

Though none go with me, I still will follow
Though none go with me, I still will follow
Though none go with me, I still will follow
No turning back, no turning back

I will be baptized and follow Jesus
I will be baptized and follow Jesus
I will be baptized and follow Jesus
No turning back, no turning back

Fourth verse by Stephen Elkins

BRIDGE OF SONG

20

WHAT DID YOU LEARN ABOUT BAPTISM? *(answers at bottom of page)*

1. Baptism has no power to _____.

2. Baptism is like "show and _____."

3. Baptism says that JESUS is _____.

4. Baptism is a _____ of Jesus.

5. Baptism requires _____.

LEARNING STATION

21

Have you **DECIDED** to follow Jesus?

· ·

Do you **BELIEVE** Jesus was baptized?

· ·

Do you **BELIEVE** He wants
His followers to be baptized?

· ·

Are **YOU** ready to be baptized?

· ·

Do you want to **"SHOW AND TELL"**
others by being baptized?

*Then tell your parents, your pastor,
or your teacher that you have
decided to follow Jesus!*

DECISION DEPOT

LORD, hear us when we PRAY:

YAHWEH, FATHER,

You have commanded that
everyone who loves you should be baptized.
I understand that baptism is like "show and tell."
When the time is right, I will be baptized to tell others
that I am a new person. Baptism will show that I love
the Lord with all my heart, soul, mind, and strength.
I know Your name, Father. May the whole world
come to know Your name, Yahweh, and that You sent
Messiah Jesus to save us. Thank You for
giving me this wonderful "show
and tell" called baptism.
Amen.

PRAYER PLACE

FIND THIS SONG
on the CD

TRAIN UP A CHILD

Train up, train up,
Train up a child in the way he should go.
Train up, train up,
Train up a child in the way she should go.
And when they are older
They will not depart from it.

**ADAPTED FROM
PROVERBS 22:6**

Words & music by Stephen Elkins

I know the LORD must love all this great singing!

And He loves you, too!

Last stop! Good-bye, everybody. *See you next time
when once again we'll choo-choo away
aboard the Gospel train and discover
all that God has for us!*

CONDUCTOR

STEVE